Expressions of Life From

The Shoebox

Author: Harvey M. Lockley

Published by: Diligence Publishing Company

Expressions of Life From The Shoebox
Copyright © 2003
Diligence Publishing
www.dpc-books.com
First Printing October 2003

Published by: Diligence Publishing Company, 41 Watchung Plaza, #239, Montclair, New Jersey 07042

Front cover design: Olson Jean-Louis, Illustrator and Graphic Artist

Cover Illustration
Copyright © 2003 by
Diligence Publishing

ISBN:0-9727416-1-5
Library of Congress Control Number: 2003095060

Printed in the United States by
Morris Publishing
3212 East Highway 30
Kearney, NE 68847
1-800-650-7888

Visit the publisher's website at www.dpc-books.com

Dedication

All proceeds obtained for the first three years from the direct sale of this book will be dedicated to an international charity.

Acknowledgements

I would like to thank those who have had and those who continue to have a direct impact in my life. I am thankful to the Lord, "Jesus Christ" for granting me wisdom and direction, especially when I wanted to live life my own selfish way. He placed situations in my life that allowed me to get back on track. To Lorie who is my friend and a beautiful, loving wife I am thankful for the wonderful relationship that we have cultivated. She allows me to be myself and supports all of my endeavors. I am grateful for my mother Barbara L. Lockley, who continues to be an inspiration to me in spite of her up hill battle with Multiple Sclerosis. She only grows sweeter with time, my sister and brother, Lynn and Tommy, because of their love, honesty and sincere concern. My extended family, because they have been such a strong support system throughout my life that I often wonder why there is a need for the term extended.

I thank God for Bishop Donald Hilliard Jr., who has been a father to me in every sense of the word since the passing of my biological father.

Throughout life and the different seasons in time, there are so many others that by influence bring these thoughts and poems to mind... to create the heart felt expressions that have been composed in this book. Please make the time to take an introspective look. Each one played a special and important role, to bring these words that will touch your heart and soul.

Attraction

Beauty
(The definition)

What is beauty?
Webster does not know...
Beauty is a smile
from your face,
what joy, to see it glow...
Glow with the warmth
that only you possess...
There is no one
quite like you,
this I must confess...
What is beauty?
Is it not plain to see?
That you are beauty,
and what beauty,
means to me.

Beauty Beyond Compare

The beauty that I see in you
is beyond compare...
It is not just your lovely smile,
your eyes or your hair...
This beauty is special
and very unique...
For this type of beauty
many men do seek...
I thank God
that I am the one
to hold and share
the beauty in you,
that is beyond compare.

Beauty
(The Search)

How can I say this?
Or what should I write?
To describe the beauty that I see
when you are in my sight...
If I searched for many days
or looked for many miles,
no where else could I find
such a pretty smile...
A smile so nice and sweet,
that it can warm the coldest heart...
In my search for such beauty,
where else would I start?
What else can I say or,
what else can I do?
But thank my heavenly Father
for a lovely young lady like you.

Deja vu

I give this rose
as a friendly gesture
to a beautiful young lady
that comes from yester.
Yester year or yesterday,
it seems as if I know you,
but I cannot really say.
Where in the past
have we ever met?
It seems that
I almost remember,
but yet I forget.
So I give this rose
as a friendly gesture,
as I try to remember
the young lady from yester.

Beauty Beyond Compare

If I had a wish or a dream
like deja vu
I could think of nothing sweeter
than spending time with you...
If women are truly made of sugar,
honey and spice...
what God has placed into other women,
He has given to you twice.
So please don't think
that I am strange
when I look at you and stare...
I am just thinking
of how God
has blessed me,
to know someone
beautiful
beyond
compare.

Sunshine
(The Unknown Lady, "On Grove Terrace")

Like Sunshine on a rainy day...
I saw her standing
in the doorway...
What a shock
and sudden surprise,
as she waved,
I smiled
and looked into her eyes...
A picture of beauty
that words
can not describe...
Only lasting for a moment
as my car drove by.
How long will this last?
What can I say?
To the Lady
who is like sunshine
on a rainy day.

Eyes of Beauty

Eyes of Beauty,
I have never seen like this...
A young Lady
so lovely
it is hard to resist...
Resist
the temptation
to stop
and stare
and say
to yourself,
"Is she really there?"
Believe it or not,
it seems to be true...
That God
made a young Lady
as Beautiful
as you.

Friendship

True Friendship

With friendship comes love,
joy and peace of mind...
And so much more
that will come with time...
It is a blessing to know
that you are a friend of mine,
because a friendship like yours
is so hard to find.

Wisdom in Choosing Relationships

I do not know you well,
but what I perceive...
Is in Christ Jesus
you love and believe...
You live your life
so that you do not hurt Him,
and that is so important
when choosing a friend.

The Guardian

To a very nice lady,
who is very sweet and kind...
If you are a friend of Aunt Helen's,
then you are a friend of mine...
I just wanted to write you
to thank you for what you have done...
Although you do not know me,
you have treated me as a son...
It is people like you
that make life worth while
and it is people like you
that make sad faces smile...

The End of A Long Distance Relationship

If I could do it all over again...
I would look for someone like you,
to have as a friend.
Life is so simple,
however we make it complex...
Planning with what we have,
not knowing
what might come next.
So we pray for guidance
and with hope and faith
we do our best,
and if we are smart,
let God handle the rest.
But as much as I would like to,
I cannot do it again.
So I am glad to have you
as a telephone friend.

Someone Nice

If someone you know
does something nice,
most of the time
you do not think twice.
If someone you do not know
extends their hand...
It really makes you wonder
and say,
"Oh man!"
As you are sitting
and wondering, why?
The thought of such kindness
brings a tear to your eye...
As you hold back the tears
and try not to cry,
you thank your
Heavenly Father
who is looking down
from the sky.

Pen Pals

When a friendship is bright
and everything is brand new,
each conversation is exhilarating...
Isn't that true?
Especially when the other person
Is special like you.
But each time I write,
in the back of my mind,
there is the thought
or the question,
of the test of time.
I quickly erase it,
because now it seems so grand,
and I say to myself,
"The test of time we will withstand."
So I continue to write
and receive each letter with joy,
like a child when he opens
a brand new toy.
And as for this friendship,
will it stay bright and brand new?
The answer to this question
is up to me
and up to you.

Deep Within

Through the thoughts
in my mind, deep within...
Someone that I have never seen
is becoming a friend...
It is difficult to grasp for,
and capture thin air...
Emotions seek refuge,
but no one is there...
Could this be
a New World order
or way to relate?
Or is this how
it should have been
since the B.C. dates?
Learning about one another
through the depths of our minds.
Building up each other
and treating people kind...
In retrospect
I sit with my hand on my chin...
Captivated by the thoughts
from deep within...

Romance

A Dream

I once had a dream
of you and me...
I once had a dream
that we would always be...
Be together,
of course,
until the end of time,
but now I can see
that it was all in my mind.
It was beautiful there
and everything was right.
I loved you endlessly,
every day and every night.
We raised a family
so loving and caring...
And if there were problems,
the burdens we were sharing.
Everything was wonderful,
we had such a happy life
and I thanked God for you,
my beautiful wife...
I once had a dream,
but do dreams really come true?
I once had a dream.
Did you have one too?

If Just, "Only For One Day"

Sometimes I imagine
a place far away...
Where we could spend some time,
if just only for one day...
A beautiful island
so warm and serene,
walking and talking together,
sharing life's dreams...
Not worried about time,
meeting deadlines,
schedules,
or important dates...
A wonderful time,
filled with peace of mind,
on this day will be our fate.
As we travel through life's maze,
for this day I await.
To spend time with you...
Just us two...
saying all that
we ever wanted to say.
I wish somehow
that it could be this way...
if just,
"only for one day."

Honey is Sweet

Honey is sweet,
but you are much sweeter
and when I hear your voice,
it warms me like a heater.
I never would have believed
that dreams could come true,
but that belief changed
the day that I met you.

Poetry is Nice

Poetry is nice,
but you are much sweeter...
and when I hear
your voice
it warms me like a heater...
A woman like you
is definitely hard to find
and I want to take a moment
to say that, "you are one of a kind."
And while I am
thinking of you
and have you on my mind.
I cannot resist,
to ask,
would you be my Valentine?

Could I Forget

Could I really forget about you?
No!
Then my poetry would be untrue...
Well then,
"Is he just playing with my mind?"
No!
I really think that
you are beautiful
and quite kind...
And every time
that I see a flower,
just like a summer shower,
thoughts of you rain in my mind,
so refreshing and
right on time.
And when the shower has ceased,
my heart and soul
are at peace.
There only I remain,
with memories of you,
that I've sustained,
so lovely is each refrain,
lingering as fragrance
after the rain.

One of a Kind

Lovely young lady
you are one of a kind...
Lovely young lady
you stay on my mind...
My love for you is like honey,
pure and sweet...
Sticky to the touch,
but even better to eat.
Who is the one
that stays on my mind?
Who is the one
that is one of a kind?
Who could be the one
that makes me feel this way?
The young lady is you
and this I must say.

Voice of Choice

If I had a choice,
it would be your voice.
The one I desire to hear,
each time the phone reaches my ear.
On the first ring I think,
who can it be?
Is it the voice
that sounds the sweetest to me?
Sweet as sugar,
no wait!
More like honey...
Just to hear from you
makes all my rainy days sunny.
To me your voice is worth
more than money.
Or even as valuable
and precious as gold,
listening to your voice
could never grow old.

Prospect of A Second Date

I once met a young lady
as pretty as can be...
I once met a young lady
that I never see...
Every now and again
when I am in my room all alone,
I hear her beautiful voice
when she rings me on the phone.
I once met a young lady
as pretty as can be...
I once met a young lady
who I wonder,
will I ever see...

The Lost Smile

It was the first time
that she spoke to me
and did not smile,
so I sat and thought about it
for a while.
What have I said?
What must I have done,
not to see the smile
that shines like the sun?
And as I sat and thought
for a while,
I hoped that this
would be the last time
that she spoke
and did not smile,
but if not,
I am sorry for
what I have done
to kill the smile that
shines like the sun.

Wonders For a Relationship

The imagination
does wonders
for a relationship...
In a moment's notice
we could be off on a trip...
To a deserted island,
cocktails for two...
A never-ending romance,
all the things that lovers do...
Imagination does wonders
for a relationship,
but as hard as I try
we're not quite there yet...
So imagination,
for now,
is as good as it gets.

Romance

How I enjoy the time
that I spend with you...
Each moment is a blessing,
so refreshing and brand new...
There is not a woman
in this world
more beautiful,
you see,
God has given this love
from you to me,
from now until eternity...
I cannot wait
for the moments
when we are together;
it is you my love
that I will always treasure.

Pretty As a Rose

As pretty as a rose,
off to work she goes...
With a smile that is one of a kind...
All of the men say,
"I wish that girl were mine."
Never seen doing anything shady,
but always carries herself like a lady.
Wherever she goes,
everyone knows
that she is the young lady
as pretty as a rose.

Thoughts of You

If I sent you a rose
for each time
that you make me smile,
the delivery trucks,
from your door,
would stretch for miles
and miles.
If every second
I received a penny,
for each wonderful thought of you,
I would be a millionaire
before the clock struck two.
I never imagined
that a blessing
could be as beautiful as you...
Someone who
loves the Lord
and wants to live Holy too...
There is always
a special feeling
when spending time with you.

Courtship

A Visit to The Aquarium

As I sat to reflect
on last weekend for a while...
Even though I was busy working,
I couldn't help but smile...
For a moment my mind wandered
to the place where I was enjoying
the beauty of God's creation
and the warmth
of His Love.
There were the fish,
the seals,
the bay with its lovely view,
but what made the day so special,
was sharing it with you.
Now, of the background noise,
I slowly became more aware...
As the vision of beauty
begins to vaporize
into thin air...
Though I held on dearly
and held on tight,
the moment slipped away,
as the daylight into the night.
Now even though the moment has left,
the memory does not end.
So I thanked God for the weekend
and for such a beautiful friend.

Can You Imagine?

You will never be able
to imagine the love
that I feel for you.
I wish that I could say
my circumstance was like,
catch twenty-two.
That would be too simple,
it is more difficult than that.
At the door of your heart,
awaits my love
like a welcome mat.
Most of the time
the sun does shine,
but when it rains,
it pours...
Yet, I will always be there waiting,
for the sound of an opening door.
You will never be able to imagine
the love that I feel for you...
Each day my love grows
more and more.
This you know is true.

Character of Christ

Like a flower
you are His fragrance,
with beauty and life.
Continue blessing others
while sharing the Spirit of Christ.
In everything that you do
and in everything that you say,
may God continue to bless you,
as you bless others this day.
As you lift your voice and sing,
may the bells of heaven ring...
Proclaiming our Lord and Savior,
Jesus Christ is King.

A Special Night

Thank you for the
most special night ever...
A night that I
will always treasure...
To meet someone
as wonderful as you...
Is to me,
like a dream come true.
Your company puts
my mind at ease,
like a cool summer's breeze
when it blows through the trees.
God knows
that I do not ever
want to see you leave.
I do not know
what happened in the past,
but I know that I want
to make this moment last.
With you in my life
I will always endeavor
to make every night for us,
"The most special night ever."

Missed Romance

We should have
been together from the start.
I knew this in my heart.
Even though we met so long ago,
you still are
oh, so beautiful.
Sweet like butter almond
with a chocolate swirl,
from the beginning,
way back then,
you should have been my girl.
Did I say girl?
Well, I surely meant Queen.
Your presence is felt like royalty
when you enter in, on the scene.
When I think upon the lost years,
my eyes fill with tears,
from the pain in my heart,
knowing we should have been together,
from the beginning and from the start.

The Plan

Was it in the plan,
that a young lady
would meet a young man?
Was it in the plan,
that he would feel
something special
when he held her hand?
Was it in the plan
that her lips would
taste so sweet,
as they kissed
holding hands
in the front car seats...?
I wish that
I knew the plan,
then we both
could understand
and I would know
just what to do,
as I am falling
in love with you.

Never Forget

Never forget
the good times that we shared.
Never forget
how much I really cared.
I cannot give you a reason
or tell you why.
All that I know,
is that you are special in my eyes.
Being with you is a special treat.
I never met someone
so kind and so sweet.
The more that I think of how
I don't want you to leave,
the more my heart becomes
pained and grieved.
I cried once before
when I thought that you would go,
by the side of my bed,
on my pillow.
And now that my pillow
is all soaked and wet,
all that I ask is that
you never forget.

Relationship

Friendship

Where does friendship start?
Where does friendship end?
For you does friendship ever begin?
Cut them down before they can walk,
shut them up before they can talk.
Like a lion after a lamb,
each one is prey to be stalked.
Give him a chance,
then turn him down...
She was there for a moment,
but now she can not be found...
Where does friendship start?
Where does friendship end?
For you does friendship ever begin?

She's Going Back Home...

Last night on my knees I cried,
then prayed for a while.
It was the first time
that I thought of you
and could not smile.
Deep in my heart
the pain was very great.
I went to a party
and stayed out late.
I was sad and felt lonely,
but didn't want to be alone,
taunted by visions of the day
that you will be gone.

Growing Together

I often pray that
you could forgive me
for some of the things
that I say and do,
as I am growing
and learning to understand you.
You are sweeter than honey,
more delicate than a rose,
a heart more precious than treasure,
with Godly love that shows.
It is plain to see
that you are as special
as special can be,
but as I am learning about you,
I am also learning about me.
Some days are beautiful,
while others are not so grand.
With prayer and faith
I must place it all in the Master's Hand,
because when no one else does know,
I know that He understands.

Letting Love Grow

Words of poetry
I wanted to send,
thanking you for
a wonderful weekend,
but maybe my timing
is now too soon.
For our love has not yet,
started to bloom.
Like a seed in the ground,
it will wait deep below
and if God is willing to water,
then, the seed will grow.
And what a beautiful thing
a seed can become,
if we stand back
and let God's will be done.
In my heart I believe
and know this is true,
because I can see
the beauty
that God has placed in you.

Is The Dating Over?

It is not often in life,
you meet someone
you really like...
Someone in life,
you would call
a husband or a wife...
It is not often in life
you meet someone
for whom you care,
whether good times
or bad times
you want to be there.
It is not often in life
that you can forget the past.
The dreams are over now,
but the memories still last.
It is not often in life,
we throw things away.
Thinking what is good
for tomorrow
is bad for today.
It is not often in life
that I meet someone like you.
I know how I feel,
but I don't know what to do.

Love's Despair

Love's Despair...
have you ever been there?
You have given it your all
to find that he or she
really doesn't care.
Doesn't care about the effort
or time that you put in...
They have different plans
for their future
and now you don't fit in,
or they tell you that
there is another...
someone that you thought
was your friend.
It is lonely like a dessert,
so much pain
and deep despair.
A miserable state
of both mind and fate,
of this place you
were so unaware.
Although you did not
come voluntarily...
Welcome to Love's Despair.

The Struggle of Love

What could I say to describe
all that we have been through?
It is better to say nothing
and to know
that there is no end to...
No end to the love,
for you that is in my heart,
even though now the distance
keeps us apart.
We must place our trust in God
and give Him our all
and He will guide our paths
and catch us if we fall.
What can I say
to describe all
that we have been through?
I will say nothing,
just know
that I will always love you...

Love Without Accord

When I hear your voice
it makes me sad
and I think of the love
that we never had.
I loved you so much,
but we could never agree.
Was it because I lacked
confidence in you
or was it your lack
of faith in me?
When I wanted it exclusive,
you thought that
we should see others.
Each time that we broke up,
the glow of love was smothered.
When you wanted to be true,
I had too many female friends.
Why couldn't we see eye to eye?
Why didn't the cycle end?
Somewhere deep inside,
deep down where it is dark,
there is a feeling
that I cannot explain
in the bottom of my heart.
So when I hear your voice
it makes me sad
and I often wonder...
How good love goes bad?

Thank You

I just wanted to take a moment
to stop and say
Thank you...
The reason that I thank you,
is for all of the wonderful
things that you do.
Not out of obligation
or because someone told you to,
but it is just an outward showing
of the beauty
inside of you.

Where is She Now?

Where is she now?
I often wonder, you know?
Even though I am better off
that our relationship did not grow.
There were too many complications
and besides it was the wrong time.
So why do thoughts of her,
continue to enter my mind?
Our love was out of desperation,
another struggle each time
that I turned around.
She was running
from her ex-boyfriend
and I was on the rebound.
But what passion and burning desire,
enough to lose your identity,
transforming like a fire
that almost put an end to me.
I am so glad to be away,
but sometimes I wish
that I was still there...
It was not all bad;
plenty of good times we did share...
Where is she now?
I often wonder, you know?
Does she think about the relationship?
Is she glad that it did not grow?

Realization of Love

I realize that you
do not feel
the way that you used to,
but this will never change
my love for you.
In life, there are many things
that you can buy,
but happiness you can not buy,
no matter how hard you try.
Time spent with you
is more than a pleasure.
Each moment with you
is like new found treasure.
I realize that you
do not feel the way
that you used to,
but one thing
that is for sure,
I will always love you.

True Love

Matter of The Heart

What does it mean
to say that I love you?
Should these words be spoken
to just a chosen few?
What does it mean
to speak this into someone's life?
And does love go away
when faced with conflict,
adversity, or strife?
So I pick up the Bible
to read John 3:16,
Hoping that I can learn,
what love really means.
You see I told someone
that I love them,
not just to play a role or part.
I told someone
that I love them,
out of the pureness of my heart.
It started off so different,
with a beauty like never before
and the Love of Jesus over shadowed it,
as the ocean does the shore.
As I read my Bible,
I find that true love is set apart...
It is not based on feelings.
It is a matter of the heart.

Change of Heart

We are three years and seven months
into the marriage relationship...
And the ties that bind the cord
have already begun to rip...
No one is at fault
and it was neither of our intention.
We were just busy
pursuing our careers and goals,
but no one stopped to mention...
Where is the unquenchable love
that we had from the start?
Why is the busyness of life
pulling us apart?
Today I will stop and take a stand....
In word and deed I will be the man...
I will restore our love with
new vigor and health
and I will place cold feelings
and selfishness back on the shelf.
Today and every day,
I must take this stand
and minute by minute,
our love will expand.
Expand to deeper depths
and higher heights...
And I will never let go,
because I am setting my sights....
One minute, seven months
and three years
now have passed
and forever we will be
and forever our love will last...

Distance

To the love of my life,
with a tear in my eye...
To the love of my life,
I try not to cry...
Miles away it seems so far,
I close my eyes for a moment,
And in my heart there you are.
Feelings of love for you so strong,
that I thirst...
So far away from you my dear,
what could be worse...
To the love of my life,
with a tear in my eye...
My love for you
will never die.

Seeking God's Will

I had intended to give you
flowers with a poem, one day
and these are the words
that the poem did say...
"You are beautiful,
sweet and lovely too
and that is why these flowers
are especially for you.
You are God fearing,
spiritually uplifting
and always kind
and that is why
thoughts of you
stay on my mind."
But the poem ends here,
for it is incomplete
and I must be sure
that it is God's will before,
again my heart speaks.
In seeking God's will
I continue to pray,
so that maybe,
I can give you
flowers with a poem,
one day.

Love's Worth

How do I say,
"I am sorry,"
for the years of pain and hurt?
How do you tell someone
that means so much,
just what their love is worth?
All that I know is
there is no one else like you
and without your love,
I do not know what I will do.
You see I have learned
so much from our past
and my love for you
will always last.
How do you tell someone
that means so much,
just what their love is worth?
It is easier to fly to Mars,
count the stars
or stop the spinning
of the earth.

What Ever!!!

I started to write a poem to you
about spending time together
and making dreams come true
and about all of the wonderful things
that we never do.
How we don't take walks
through the park
while holding hands
or sit on the beach
with our toes in the sand.
Listening to the ocean
as the waves come closer and closer.
When two people are involved
you know that they are supposed to...
Supposed to work together
to do the things that they like.
Sometimes things go wrong,
but more than not,
they will go right.
So I am writing you a poem
about spending time together.
I am asking you to make an effort
and not to just say,
"What ever!!!"

The True Valentine

It is February fourteenth
and I am back with a rhyme,
on a day that they remember
a man called Valentine.
But this rhyme is different,
as you will soon see,
because it is dedicated to
Someone who really loves me.
Loves me so much,
more than anyone dares,
because it was
Him on the cross
when I should have been there.
What more could be done
to show that He really cares.
If more proof is needed,
He has taken the time
to count my hairs.
So on February fourteenth,
a day called Valentine's,
I am asking You,
Lord Jesus,
Would you be mine?

Real Love

I want to take the time
to express the way that I feel.
It is not easy using words
to show that my love is real.
I must have been crazy
and out of my head
to do what I have done
and say the things I have said...
In a few weeks I have learned
so much about life
and the pain that I feel
cuts me like a knife.
What I want to say,
is that you mean the world to me
and I don't know why I was so blind
that this I could not see.
If I were to lose you,
not only would I cry,
if I were to lose you,
then part of me would die.
And half of a man
equals less than a boy.
And half of a man
means a life with out joy.
The love inside of me
that I want to share with you
will be ten times greater
than you ever thought or knew.

If I Were A Rose

If I were a rose,
with thoughts of things to do,
my thought would be...
to be held by you.
Next placed in a vase,
filled by you with water
and I would smile
from petal to petal
as I was placed in order.
My days would be spent
giving you the most beautiful scent,
in an attempt to make your life
much more pleasant.
And at the end before I die...
You would see my petals cry...
One by one they would drop,
as tears that never stop.
Because, if I were a rose,
with thoughts of things to do,
my first thought would be...
To always be there for you.

My Wife

To my beautiful,
beautiful wife.
You are the woman
who completes my life.
No one else makes me happy
the way that you do
and I truly thank and praise,
the Lord for you.
If my love were edible
like fine wine,
every taste would show
that it grows stronger
and sweeter with time.
Together the Lord has brought us
and together we shall stay,
until we are caught up to meet Him
on that very special day.

Our Love

Just thinking of you
and our love so true...
Especially how God
has made it brand new...
In Him we must live
and always stay strong.
Then our love will thrive
and surely last long,
Because together you and I
have always belonged.
Just thinking of you
and our love so true...
Isn't it wonderful?
The things that God can do...

Spirituality

An Answer to Prayer

When my spirit was down
and troubling me,
God brought into my life
a young lady named Lorie.
Her beauty is more
than in body, spirit and mind.
I knew from the beginning
that she was a treasure
and quite a find.
With the loveliest voice,
both gentle and sweet,
conversation with Lorie
is definitely a treat.
She makes my heart happy,
Lord you know that this is true,
but most of all Father
she has her eyes set on You.
Once my spirit was down
and troubling me,
but now,
I thank You Lord
for sending Lorie.

Thank You Father

I thank You, Heavenly Father
for everything that, You have done...
I thank You, Heavenly Father
for sending down Your Son...
I thank You, Heavenly Father,
because, You have chosen me
and I thank You, that, from all my sins,
You have set me free.
Even though there are times
when I want to do things my way,
get caught up in the world
and tend to go astray.
You have always been there
when I realized that I was wrong.
You have always been there,
so gentle, yet so strong.
You have always been there
when I thought that I was missing out
and with Your loving Word,
You have erased all my fears and doubts.
You help me to be sure when
I do not know which path to take.
Trusting in You Lord,
has never been a mistake.
So I thank you Heavenly Father,
for every thing, that, You have done.
I thank you Heavenly Father
in the name of Jesus Christ, Your Son.

Love So Grand

I never would have imagined
that love could be so grand,
with so many little intricacies,
of which all,
I do not understand.
Like when I am moved
with feelings of love,
"what should I do?"
Do I share the feelings with God
or do I share the feelings with you?
So we look to Christ who saved us
and we remember
what we have been shown...
I no longer belong to me,
but I am part
of the living stone.
I give it all to Jesus,
for I know that he understands,
because sharing love
is a beautiful thing
when we place it
in God's hands.

In My Savior's Hand

Life goes so fast,
but time goes so slow.
How will I spend my time?
Only God knows.
Second by second
the hours tick away,
it is tomorrow now,
so what will I do today?
I wait for the end of the week
for the fruits of my labor.
It seems as if everyone has to get some,
nothing left for me to savor.
It takes so long to reach the goals
that you set, as your life slips away.
Three steps forward,
two steps back
is the routine every day.
The things that I long for
money can not buy,
true love from God,
for this my heart cries.
But money is the means
for substance and gain,
and money is the cause
of unnecessary pain.
Life goes so fast,
but time goes so slow...
With my hand in Yours Lord,
is the only way that I know.

The Christmas Card

Christmas is a wonderful season
this is true.
But what really makes it special
is having friends like you.
May God and His love
bless you every day
and may you continue to love others
in a very special way.
Christmas is a wonderful season,
this is very true.
Our prayer is
that you will experience
God's love, joy and peace
in everything that you do.

All Hail!

All hail the great fool!
He would risk his salvation
to do what he thought was cool.
It would begin with a thought
conjured up in his mind,
some of them mean, some nasty,
some evil and some unkind.
Knowing in his heart
that it would just be a matter of time,
before the thought was reality
with sensations like fine wine.
Those tantalizing feelings
that satisfy my mind.
He could execute each plan perfectly,
without a doubt,
getting further and further
from God and leaving Jesus out.
All hail the great fool!
Life is surely treating him cruel.
He no longer looks to his Lord in the sky
and as he stops and wonders why, he cries.
More confused than ever,
because his new master is tricky and clever.
Will his life end this way?
He hopes the answer is... "Never."
All hail the great fool!
Will he ever change his path?
All hail the great fool!
Living the life you lead,
you won't last.

Reflections

The Lonely Ones

Where do all of the lonely people go?
If you saw them,
would you even know?
All are lonely for different reasons,
some just because it is lonely season.
You see them in crowds,
but oh, so lonely.
Keeping their composure,
trying not to appear homely.
Some are with friends
and some are with a spouse,
you can almost guarantee,
there is one in every house.
It is so hard to tell,
they never open up...
They stay behind their lonely walls
like liquid in a cup.
Where do all of the lonely people go?
Please tell me if you dare,
or are these people lonely
because people like you don't care?

Patience

Patience is a virtue...
But there are some times
I feel that I cannot wait.
I want it all!!!
Right now,
delivered First Class,
with a post mark
of yesterday's date...
Somehow I know
that this is not right,
how much can you self gratify?
If you over water a flower,
soon the plant will die...
Patience is a virtue...
Sometimes the waiting
makes me want to cry...
But since patience is a virtue...
to be patient
I will try.

Time to Unwind

Why can't I relax and unwind?
The time that I find to be mine
is never really mine.
Some have time for leisure
to spend with family...
Some go for walks
and talks in parks
and play among the trees...
No matter how I try
this doesn't work for me.
There is always work to do
or a task that I did not see.
Why can't I unwind and relax?
My plate is always
filled to the max.
Each day of business
pushes me closer
and closer to the brink.
My day of relaxation is coming
sooner than you think.

Beyond High School

What are you going to do
when the struggle is over?
Adolescence is gone
and you are a little older...
What are you going to do
now with your life?
Will you get a job?
Will you find a husband or a wife?
All of your friends have gone away
and are doing what they do best.
So what are you going to do,
to keep from making your life a mess?
As I look over my shoulder,
the realization has just begun,
what it means to be older,
though there are many victories
that I have won.
For me the struggle of life,
has really just begun.

Grand Pa

What is life like for Grand Pa?
He is ninety-two plus three...
And though he has known me
all of my life
he does not remember me...
What is life like for Grand Pa?
As he sits there in a chair...
Every utterance
once meant so much,
but now does anyone care?
What is life like for Grand Pa?
Ponder this if you dare,
because one day
just like Grand Pa,
you will soon be there.

Bleed With Emotion

I bleed with emotion
when I think about the past,
and love so strong,
that did not last.
Every day was a new situation
to continually work my nerves.
The relationship had so much action
it could have been a verb.
But that is what made it bitter sweet...
Feelings so strong
a love so deep.
We lived for the moments
of meeting face to face...
and the exhilarating
sensation of the tender embrace...
Through all the joy and pain,
there was deep intimacy
that we would share...
Such passionate fire
and burning desire,
was too much
for any soul to bare...
Nothing else seemed to matter
and if it did, we didn't care...
I bleed with emotion
when I think about the past...
A love so strong
Why could it not last?

A Reflection of The Past

Years have passed,
yet I keep thinking back...
Upon the words
that were expressed
and how they still impact...
Impact what I do
and the things that I say,
as if we were still together,
on yesterday.
Was it really so bad
that we had to separate?
Then how is it, from the past,
we still communicate?
In a moment when I
am caught off guard,
a thought, by something,
is triggered.
A vivid scene from then,
is now, slowly reconfigured.
A radiant picture
of how it once was...
At the height of our time,
at the peak of our love...
Streams of emotion
rush from my heart,
as I attempt to stop them
before the bleeding starts.
Years have passed
yet my mind still goes back.
But in reality, I know
that I could not do that...

The Predicament of Man

She will never understand...
And, No!!!!
I am not going to use my hand...
Once a month is not enough
and if we miss that,
it really gets rough.
I never thought that marriage
could be so tough...
Everything else is really great,
though in my mind
I contemplate,
and it gets worst
at night when it is late,
as I wait for a change of fate,
while I am thinking
of my lovely mate,
but the only thing that changes
is the date.
Yet, for her life is grand,
but she will never understand
the predicament of man.

A Visit to The Nursing Home

I used to visit my Grandfather,
amidst the people there...
That no one bothered to visit,
or even really cared...
A sea of old souls
awaiting a very special ship,
that will carry them on a journey
known as life's final trip.
While at the shore of souls,
there was a Lady that I would see.
This very special Lady
was named Mrs. Duduley.
How pleasant and sweet were her words,
which portrayed her state of bliss,
with undertones of pain,
that you could not miss.
We would talk about days of her past,
the conversation would not long last,
then she would pause and say,
"I look forward to that day
and how great it will be,
when Captain Jesus comes,
here to rescue me".
As pain would fill my heart
and water my eyes,
I would leave to avoid the tears
that I would soon cry.
As I would let go of her hand
and walk out of view,
I could hear her trembling voice,
Saying, continually, "I love you."

The Need

Why is it never satisfied?
The more that I give it
the more that it tries...
Tries to find ways
to fulfill its needs.
Like the fuel of a fire,
on others it feeds.
It never really gives me rest
or peace of mind,
seemingly for a little while,
that only lasts a short time.
Then it returns
with strength and
new found power,
if not placed under
the Lord's subjection,
I am sure to be devoured.
Why is it,
that it is never satisfied?
Because while feeding it daily,
behind reality I try to hide.

Suck It Up

Late at night I breathe in deep...
I suck it up
before I sleep...
I suck it up
and hold up my chin...
I suck it up.
I do it for them...
They live their lives
as happy as can be...
The pain inside of me,
I will never let them see...
The thoughts in my head,
I cannot share...
Rain on their parade?
I wouldn't dare...
A new day is dawning,
time to do it again...
I suck it up,
and keep smiling...

A Side of Me

There is a side of me
that likes to dream...
Of each and every
possible imagination it seems...
Romance on an island
or the king of some new land.
A world with total peace,
where each race,
walks hand and hand...
There is a side of me
that keeps asking,
"why?"
With all your might
you may try,
but your dreams pass you by...
These fantastic thoughts
you conjured up in your mind
and there they will stay,
until the end of time.
There is a side of me
that won't say, "No"...
Not willing to let the dreams die,
not willing to let go...
So each day is a piece of the puzzle,
like a movie on a picture screen,
putting my dreams together
until the full picture can be seen.

Compilation

Sharing Kisses

Oh, how it hurts
to know that she
is sharing her kisses.
Someone else is catching
all of the ones that he misses.
At those beautiful lips...
He loves it when he is there,
but when he is away;
those lips are being shared.
How much more can he take?
Who will stop the heartache?
How long will these
nightmares last?
Or will this,
sharing a kiss,
be a thing of the past?
For I dreamed those
kisses were special,
but now alas,
this dream is one
that is fading fast.

Abortion

Let's take a moment
to say a rhyme for the dead.
To keep alive the
thoughts of our children,
as memories in our heads...
Knowing that each time it happens,
I wish it were me instead.
Let's take a moment
to say a rhyme for the dead.
For each voice
that will never be heard,
and each word
that will never be said.
Each time for the executions
and the money that was spent,
knowing that all of Gods children
are truly heaven sent.
I think sometimes,
how beautiful it would have been...
Making a wife of a life long friend.
Will it ever happen?
Only God knows,
but right now,
in my head,
the cry of our children grows.
In saying all of this,
what have I really said?
But let's take a moment
and remember the dead.

More Than Conversation

Relating with you
provokes me to think...
Then the realization of my thoughts,
comes by a pen,
through the ink...
Contemplation of our lives,
as it relates to the things that matter.
Conversation with you darling,
is more than superficial chatter...
So as I pour another cup
from the fountain of intellect...
I drink, while I think,
upon the words that you project...

Lorie

Often times I think of how
God has blessed me,
by meeting you...
For this I thank Him
and Praise His name too.
If beauty could be measured
there is one thing that holds true...
There is not a big enough ruler
to measure
all of the beauty
possessed in you.
You always have
an encouraging word to say.
Conversation with you
always makes my day,
but most of all,
with you I like spending time.
You are a light in the world,
a beam of sunshine.

Another Poem

I wrote another poem,
but this one,
no one,
can see...
It's classified confidential,
because it exposes
the inner me...
The human character
can be astounding
and too much for another to bear...
Information in the wrong hands
can be used to set a trap
or a snare...
I wrote another poem,
and this one,
no one,
can see...
I wrote another poem,
and I wrote it
just for me...

Order Form

Use this convenient order form to order additional copies of
Expressions Of Life From
The Shoebox

Please Print:

Name_____

Address_____

City_____ **State** _____

Zip Code _____

Phone (**)**_____

_____ copies of book @ $11.95 each $_____

Postage and handling @ $2.95 per book $_____

NJ residents add .72 tax per book $_____

Total amount enclosed $_____

Make checks payable to
Diligence Publishing Company

Send to Diligence Publishing Company
41 Watchung Plaza #239
Montclair, NJ 07042

Or visit us online at:
http://www.DPC-Books.com

Thank You!